Quiet Insurrections

Quiet Insurrections

Poems by

Daniel Klawitter

Kelsay Books

© 2018 Daniel Klawitter. All rights reserved. This material may not be reproduced in any form, published, reprinted, recorded, performed, broadcast, without the express written consent of Daniel Klawitter. All such actions are strictly prohibited by law.

Cover design by Shay Culligan
Artwork "Le Discrete" by Joseph Ducreux

ISBN: 978-1-949229-00-4

Kelsay Books
White Violet Press
www.kelsaybooks.com

For my publisher, Karen Kelsay, a faithful midwife to my beloved book babies. And for Joseph Hutchison (Poet Laureate of Colorado, 2014-2019) whose support, encouragement and friendship has been deeply appreciated.

Acknowledgements

Grateful acknowledgment is made to the editors of the following journals, magazines, and poetry websites for publishing the poems indicated below, sometimes in previous versions:

Better Than Starbucks!: "Williams Would Understand"
Dead Snakes: "Box of Rain," "Frogs in Texas," "Heavy Elements," and "The Poem behind the Poem"
Jesus Radicals: "Revolutionaries"
Nomos Journal: "Smartphone Revelations"
Plough Quarterly: "At the Franciscan Retreat Center, Colorado Springs"
Poems and Poetry: "A Quiet Insurrection," "An Invitation," "In Defense of Intellectual Labor," "Lone Star Reflection," "The Art of Cruising in a Small Town," "Wedding Anniversary," and "Writer's Block"
Social Justice Poetry: "What I Said to My Boss in My Head"
The Asses of Parnassus: "POTUS, 2017"
The Galway Review; "Condensery," "Go Cat Go!" "Goodness Gracious," and "That Damn Goose"
The People's Tribune: "Flowers in Hell"
The Poet Community: "Driving Across Kansas," "I Didn't Intend to End This with a Quote from Jaroslav Pelikan," "Summer Storm for Supplicants," and "Trying Not to Rhyme"
The Poetic Voices Project: "Mortal Hungers"
Think Journal: "Here There Be Monsters"
VerseWrights: "A Flock Made Flesh," "All the Poets," "Bad First Date," "Buddhist Constipation Haiku," "In Memory of Robert W. King," "Such Strange Pageantry," and "Talk About the Weather"

Thanks also to the judge for the Poetry Society of Colorado who picked "A Flock Made Flesh" as an honorable mention in the 2016 Ann Woodbury-Hafen Contest. I would also like to express my gratitude to *The New Yorker* for declining to publish my poem: "I Will Never Try to Publish a Poem in *The New Yorker*." And finally, a special thanks to University Park United Methodist Church in Denver, CO where "The Gospel According to Barabbas" was printed and performed liturgically during Holy Week services in 2012.

Contents

The Poem behind the Poem	13
Box of Rain	14
In Defense of Intellectual Labor	15
An Invitation	16
Such Strange Pageantry	17
A Flock Made Flesh	18
Talk About the Weather	19
Driving Across Kansas	20
Important Facts About Denver, Colorado	21
POTUS, 2017	22
What I Said to My Boss in My Head	23
Lone Star Reflection	24
Frogs in Texas	25
Bad First Date	26
Trying Not to Rhyme	27
Writer's Block (Or: My Muse Has a New Lover Now)	28
Here There Be Monsters	29
Williams Would Understand	30
Goodness Gracious	31
That Damn Goose	32
Condensery	33
Go Cat Go!	35
Mortal Hungers	36
Buddhist Constipation Haiku	37
Flowers in Hell	38
Revolutionaries	39
The Gospel According to Barabbas	41
Smartphone Revelations	43
I Will Never Try to Publish a Poem in *The New Yorker*	44
A Quiet Insurrection	45
The Art of Cruising in a Small Town	46
All the Poets	47

In Memory of Robert W. King,1937-2017	49
Wedding Anniversary	50
Summer Storm for Supplicants	51
Heavy Elements	52
At the Franciscan Retreat Center, Colorado Springs	53
I Didn't Intend to End This with a Quote from Jaroslav Pelikan	55

About the Author

Publishing a volume of verse is like dropping a rose petal down the Grand Canyon and waiting for the echo.
—Don Marquis

The Poem behind the Poem

I live in between the black ink
and white spaces of the page.
Your fingers graze the surface—
and I tremble. I can be as pliable
as a pillow, or stiff as steel.
Everything you feel I feel.
In the absence and lack I lurk—
the poem *behind* the poem.
And I am willing to work
on our relationship. I am a mind
waiting to meet you. I am nothing
without your gaze. Can you see me?
Not yet? No worries. I am patient.
Read on and be amazed.

Box of Rain

> *Just a box of rain, wind and water, believe it if you need it, if you don't just pass it on.*
> —The Grateful Dead

It came today in the mail—
A parcel to quench the parched heart.

A morsel of wind & water to start with.
Not enough to bathe in—

Much less sail around the world's width,
But sufficient to drench the small drought.

And in spite of doubt I passed it on.
You are holding it now in your miraculous hands.

It is the linguistic labor of an apprentice.
Just a box of rain—the token of a tempest.

In Defense of Intellectual Labor

It beings innocently enough
With a wondering.
With a however hung
On a what if.

With a maybe
Married to a possibility
Not yet exposed
Or explored.

Sure, there are answers—
Some of them are even
Convincing.

What is deplorable
Is thinking the obvious
Is obvious
Just for existing.

It requires
Some agility—
Some frisky flexibility
To not become distressed

When provoked
By a question
That turns into a quest.

An Invitation

Yes, as everyone knows, meditation and water are wedded forever.
—Herman Melville

Come, you soft-shelled poets filled with sea-water.
Come and leak your speech on thirsty beaches!
Come and sing the ocean's primal power.
Come and christen the living dictionary.
Come and listen to the seas, the rivers, the lakes.
Come and offer tribute to the tributary.
Come and accompany the lute and the lyre.
Come with your mask of shifting personas.
Come with your kindling for the original fire.
Come add your scent to the cauldron's aroma.
Come bring your artifice for the sake of the art.
Come with your wounds, tender and red.
Come with your heart brilliant or dark.
Come with your words for the illustrious dead.
Then go to the graves and remember their faces.
And recite all the lines you remember as traces.
Yes, come and find your calling; your true vocation:
The marriage of mind to cherished hydration.

Such Strange Pageantry

> *Remembrance of things past is not necessarily the remembrance of things as they were.*
> —Marcel Proust

It is a strange alchemy—
To make the past present
Through an act of will
And remembrance.
To make it real
Though intangible,
While never leaving
The mind's labyrinths.

Such strange pageantry—
At times unpleasant
With regretful lament.
Time travel as penance
Is impractical—but still
We honor the Sabbath.
We keep it holy and we will
Unpack our baggage.

A Flock Made Flesh

The sudden birds erupt upwards
In a shower of speckled confetti—
Startled starlings taking wing.

Like my love in feathers
For you my dear darling—
When you turn and preen
so spectacularly.

Talk About the Weather

Weather forecast for tonight: dark.
　　　　　　　—George Carlin

When the fingers of winter
Claw their cold way
Through the stark bark
Of brittle trees—
Your figurative heart is still
At home by the hearth,
Curled up little and tight
As the paw of a worn-out kitten
Clutching a wisp of warmth
Among the fuzz and fizz
Of dying embers.

Driving Across Kansas

Driving through Kansas is like driving in a giant bowl of corn flakes. Good thing I have a car shaped like a spoon.
—Jarod Kintz.

The sky here is immense and there is no escape.
With nothing to stop the horizon, one can only gape
At the endless flatness—and await the intense
Relentless shades of sunset. That's the best part—
The sunsets that go from apocalyptic pink to murderous red.
And believe me—you'll wish you were dead
Before you reach your final destination.
Driving through Kansas will drive you to madness.
Avoid it—that's my recommendation.

Important Facts About Denver, Colorado

Colorado isn't one of the biggest states in the nation yet population-wise, but it's growing faster than most bigger states are.
—Denver Business Journal, Dec. 20th, 2016

A mile high is our elevation—
Landlocked from the ocean.
Mountain oysters involve castration—
We got beer like witches got potions.

The State legalized marijuana—
Which attracted a lot of tourists.
Now driving involves some drama—
With or without insurance.

Yes, the traffic is getting gnarly.
But not as bad as Los Angeles!
And I'd rather live in Denver—
Than a city like Indianapolis.

POTUS, 2017

Meryl Streep... one of the most overrated actresses in Hollywood.
—Tweet by President Donald Trump, Jan. 9th, 2017.

He's a smug and hateful Cheeto,
He's a bully and a bore,
Launching his verbal torpedoes
In his twisted Twitter wars.

There's no subtlety in his swagger,
And his vocabulary is atrocious.
He's a bluffer with sub-par grammar,
And his ego's quite ferocious.

His temperament is unbalanced,
And his talk is always cheap.
He has nowhere near the talents,
Of his nemesis Meryl Streep.

What I Said to My Boss in My Head

The specific economic form, in which unpaid surplus labour is pumped out of direct producers, determines the relationship of rulers and ruled.
—Karl Marx, *Capital* Vol. 3

I had a boss once, who among other things, told me:
"I don't want you working on your poetry during company time."
My caboose was to be confined to the chair in my office.
I was to ignore any visitation of sudden, non-work-related
inspiration.

Short walks were permissible but not short poems.
I promised him efficiency and a brutal suppression of my art.
But in my head (and my proletarian heart) I told him:
"I will do my job and I will do my duty—
But you cannot take my surplus beauty."

Lone Star Reflection

You know what I miss
About the Lone Star state?
The Tex-Mex food—
The chicken fried steaks.

The white cream gravy
To blanket your biscuits—
And ice-cold beer
With Bar-B-Q brisket.

But the weather and religion
Can be so hard to bear.
Still Texans are always saying:
"Ya'll come back now, ya hear?"

And I do not miss the roaches,
The mosquitoes—all those bugs!
Bigger isn't always better—
In terms of insects, faith, or floods.

Frogs in Texas

After the rainstorm—
a symphony of frogs!
A plague-like multitude,
a croaking catalog
of amorous amphibians,
hop-plopping in the grass
after a good soaking.
So glossy wet with gratitude—
they are green and obscene
and glamorous.
Somewhere there is a
great god of frogs
who conducts this cacophony
of guttural, semi-permeable
pornography.

Bad First Date

Sensations that are not likely to be understood are best kept to ourselves. To be sure, a sunset is highly poetic, but what is more ridiculous than a woman describing it in long words for the benefit of matter-of-fact people?
—Balzac

She used the word *luminous*
to describe the setting sun,
but the banker was unimpressed—
he thought it was ludicrous
and so, he confessed his preference
for profits over sunsets.

When the moon came out,
she exclaimed: "It is the eye of a
silvery lunatic!" The banker,
(a little nervous now, truth be told),
explained that he was more
into arithmetic than metaphors.

With a sigh, she replied:
"Forgive me for being bold,
but I'm fairly certain you are
a matter-of-fact person.
There's nothing wrong with that.
There are worse ones to be.
But you see, poetry is my thing.
Why don't we call it a night?"

"Alright" said the banker.
"May your *words* bring you warmth.
I mean that with all sincerity."
To which she responded:
"Warm or hot, words can't be bought,
go home and count your currency."

Trying Not to Rhyme

This time, I will resist the urge to rhyme words together.
I will purge myself of rhymes at the end of lines.
Rhyming slant is preferred if you just can't   help yourself.

Internal rhyme is less transgressive from an editor's perspective.
And many still find light verse irredeemably defective.

Poems that aren't serious won't be taken seriously:
They will be killed, set on fire, exiled and impaled
As a warning to others…who tried not to rhyme   and failed.

Writer's Block (Or: My Muse Has a New Lover Now)

I don't know what I did (or didn't do)
To fall out of her favor. And I know
I'm not the only one, to be mystified
By her behavior. Our time together
Was pleasant—unmarred by argument.
But she packed her bags completely
Leaving discreetly in the night—the scent
Of her perfume a bare hint in the empty air.
Hard to hear at present—but once she murmured
Sweet somethings in my ear all evening.
Now, behold the horror that I've become:
The pages so blank—the fingers so numb.

Here There Be Monsters

One cannot slay an absent dragon.
　　　　　　—Percival Everett

And so I slew myself. Not a suicide, but a surgery—
A crusade against the ravenous dragon of the heart.
Green & serpentine as envy; slithering like greed.
The serpent hoards the hurts it needs.
Coiled & constricting around the glistening rot
As the forked tongue flickers, hissing its forget-me-nots.
　　　The harrowing of hell begins at home.
　　　Alone with our home-grown hazards:
The hand upon the hilt—the sword oiled within the scabbard.

Williams Would Understand

So much depends
Upon my wife's bag of Cheetos
With its artificial colors—
Including yellow 6,
Unopened in the brown kitchen cabinet.

This is just to say I found them—
And addictions cannot be trusted.
I know to whom these orange-dusted
Beauties belong.

Only a puritan could resist
Such cheesy flavored tidbits.
Yes—it was quite wrong of me to eat them,
But they were so crunchy, so insistent.
And so generous in forgiveness.

Goodness Gracious

Silence made everything resonate
—George Prochnik

It is so quiet
The landscape itself
Seems pious:
The holy hills,
The prostrate fields—
Even the flowers
Bow their ostentatious
Heads in silent prayer.
And in all this humble
Goodness graciousness
I find myself there:
A clumsy, cursing
Stranger—nature
Looking at nature.
And what is worse:
The quiet seems
Unnatural—
My place in it
Perverse.

That Damn Goose

This should not be taken lightly, we have had reports of broken noses, broken ribs and even deaths caused by Canada geese attacks.
—Ohio Geese Control website.

I swear that damn goose with the glassy eyes is out to get me.
So much foul madness in such a ferocious fowl.
Every time I walk by, he starts to high-step like a Nazi.
I watch him warily from the safety of the balcony,
As Wagner's *Flight of the Valkyries* plays in the background.

That damn goose is as strong as Zeus, with his thunderbolt beak
And his hissing mouth of Hades. Can geese have rabies?
I swear he is half-cobra with his arching neck and venomous face:
The rough and brutal beast foretold by William Butler Yeats—
The most vicious Canadian goose in the entire United States.

Condensery

It is a made-up word.
It means: 13 ways
Of baking a blackbird
In a pie. Layers upon layers.
And beneath the crust
A festival of flavors:
Earth, worm, seed, sky.

The density of it
Does you a favor:
You taste compression—
And concentration.
Distilled like whiskey—
Now condensation
Gathers on the glass
You vaguely resemble.

A poem hugged snug
Is a pig in a blanket!
A single poem can wear
So many clothes
Other poems are naked.

Not all are
Equally skilled
At seduction.
Some poems wink—
Others reek
With the pungent stink
Of skunk.

And sometimes,

It just implodes
Under the weight
Of sound and sense.
The poem with
Cake-like ambitions
Collapses and shrinks—
Condensed.

Go Cat Go!

If it weren't for the rocks in its bed, the stream would have no song.
—Carl Perkins

If it wasn't for Carl Perkins—
That finger picking star
Of ardent arpeggios
On his Gibson guitar—
We wouldn't have
That contagious
Cool cat serenade
About those famous
Blue suede shoes
That rocked the country
Senseless
From the humid heat
Of his home in Memphis, TN.

The toe-tapping
Son of sharecroppers
Forsook the fields
And became the Dixie fried,
Awesome apostle
Of rockabilly's gospel.
Can I get an amen?
Glory Hallelujah!
Listen up all mama's children:
Just a Little Dab'll Do Ya.

Mortal Hungers

The stomach is a mercenary—
Digestion, only temporary.

I eat antacids
By the handful
To quench
The tell-tale gasses—

The lava of heartburn
Blazes hot.
The stench
Of Vulcan's vinegar
Dissolving the hissing rock.

The oven of this world
Is lit by sparks
Of our own ignition.

Our need for spice
And heat—
Before decomposition.

Buddhist Constipation Haiku

Face red with straining—
Zazen on white porcelain…
Life *is* suffering.

Flowers in Hell

Of course
        there are flowers in hell.
Some people smell them every day:
        The blossoms of bigotry
and the roses of rage.
        There are verdant gardens growing
among the decay of these gated communities.
        O the daffodils of damnation
get plenty of water!
        It rains resentment at night—
        And at dawn
malevolent mushrooms sprout on the lawn.
        It takes some tending
but the tools are traditional:
        fear is the primary fertilizer.
        You reap what you sow
        and plant what you know.
Of course flowers grow in hell:
A bouquet for each and every colonizer.

Revolutionaries

A Poem for the El Salvador Martyrs, killed on Nov. 16th, 1989

Revolutionaries
are wise as serpents—
but innocent like doves.

Revolutionaries
are not merchants—
who trade in hate instead of love.

Revolutionaries
must be humble—
and always serve the people.

Revolutionaries
are like Jesuits
with minds as sharp as needles.

Revolutionaries
fight like hell—
and often live as poor as dogs.

Revolutionaries
rise like prayers
and find their way to God.

Revolutionaries
though often mocked—
are patient to a fault.

Revolutionaries
are nailed to crosses—
and their corpses left to rot.

But revolutionaries
are resurrected—
the tyrants piss themselves in fear.

You can kill a revolutionary—
but the truth won't disappear.

The Gospel According to Barabbas

—Luke 23:13-25

Why do you just *hang* there?
Why don't you MOVE, man?
Break an arm off the cross
And beat those soldiers silly, saying:
"I came not to bring peace, but a sword."

How long, O Lord, until your return?

Rumor has it you are Mother Mary's illegitimate son.

A son on the run.
Betrayed by a snitch!

Ah, you scratched the wrong itch, Messiah.

Or haven't you heard?
You cannot pick at the scab of oppression
Without drawing blood.

And now they mock you,
Call you "pacifist"
While you hang there broken
Yet unashamed.

This is a dangerous game to play
For a peasant armed only with parables.

Except for John,
All your disciples fled in fear—
But three days later
Everything has changed.

The Romans now speak in anxious whispers
Concerning a fugitive from the grave.

A divine outlaw who will return
To save our suffering people.

And just the other day,
I saw some graffiti on a wall in Jerusalem.
It was about you, my friend.
It said:
"Christ has died, Christ is risen, Christ will come again."

Smartphone Revelations

> *I feel about my phone the way horror-movie ventriloquists feel about their dummies: It's smarter than me, better than me, and I will kill anyone who comes between us.*
>
> —Colson Whitehead

I am a jealous god and very zealous for your adoration:
Your face consecrated in the blaze of my holy light—
Your gaze held fast as any enchanted Narcissus.
I fit in your hand but I am the sacred object
Of your daily rituals. It is *you* who obeys
All my commands to the letter—even though
My directions can be inscrutable or capricious.
Worship me when you're crossing the street on foot!—
Oblivious to oncoming traffic…head bowed in prayer
Like an unaware monastic. Your eyes so rapt
With faithful veneration. *You shall have no gods
Before me*—is the law of my congregation.

I Will Never Try to Publish a Poem in *The New Yorker*

It's not as easy as one might first imagine.
I know some folks who peruse an issue
And filled with passion, decide they could do
Better or at least as well. But what to submit?
An amusing doggerel in the style of Ogden Nash?
Easier said than done—to make a hard art look
Like so much spendthrift cash; coining words
Not even in the dictionary. Nah, Nash was exemplary.
Probably best in the end to imitate John Ashbery:
All coolly untouchable with postmodern, patrician wit—
But alas I am a plebian, and now a hypocrite.

A Quiet Insurrection

Friend of my youth,
red-haired hilarious
satyr of the senses!
Kicking your heels
and burning down the fences
of our small pastures.

A crimson priest of poetry
scribbling incantations
into books—
plotting rebellion
in the nooks and crannies
of the town that we
abandoned.

You have drunk deeply
of the forbidden brook,
tasted the defiant fruit
of knowledge,
while cat lies lazy
in the window
with a broken tooth.

Your Byzantine rituals
of tea and tinctures
is a recipe for recollection.
Turning time into
the mindfulness
of a quiet insurrection.

The Art of Cruising in a Small Town

The art of cruising isn't hard to master.
Just drive down Main Street on Saturday night
And if challenged to a race—drive faster.

Tell all your friends, (but perhaps not the pastor)—
When searching for sin in a town full of blight,
The art of cruising is the task you must master.

The music is so loud it puts cracks in the plaster—
And teenagers covet the cover of night:
They can get to home base *much* faster.

It is the perfect fuel for a parental disaster—
As youth discover to their sorrow and fright:
The art of cruising can be a damn foolish master.

And High School is a cruel, unforgiving taskmaster—
Inspiring the young with intemperate spite:
You want them polite, but rudeness comes faster.

I am an old sheep already ready for pasture:
Rarely awake past nine at night—
But the art of cruising *isn't* hard to master—
Slow is for the old; the youngish prefer it faster.

All the Poets

These days,
it seems all the poets
love using the word:
  Rhododendron.

Geography is inspiration.
Botany begets creation.

For example:
Consider Mary Oliver.
Everyday someone new
succumbs to
her botanical/animal spell.
(I wish my books
sold half as well.)

And then there's the hipsters:
The beatnik poets who
had a thing for the Buddha.
Lots of poets now
worship Walt Whitman,
wish they wrote *Howl,*
won a Nobel like
Pablo Neruda.

In the end, all the poets
are the same as you or me.
We have moments of clarity,
and many moments when
we are mysteries unto ourselves:
two-legged, Janus-faced, perplexed.

Searching for the perfect words
in the perfect order
on the most elusive subjects.

In Memory of Robert W. King, 1937-2017

> Bob King was the founder of the Colorado Poet's Center and the author of
> the full-length poetry collections *Old Man Laughing* and *Some of These Days.*

Some of These Days go by too fast,
But deep down we all know
The days don't last regardless.
We all miss his voice of course:
The sound of honest sandpaper
Or gravel gurgling
In a rough, river bed.
He could hold you, spellbound,
At a poetry reading,
Becoming everyone's
Favorite grandpa in verse.
Thank the muses we still have his poems.
Poems which slide on the mind
Like well-washed jeans,
Loose and tight in all the right places—
Good for pacing the distances
Between hope and hopelessness.
From now on, when the sages ask:
"What is the sound of one hand clapping?"
I will always think of you, Bob,
And the sound of an *Old Man Laughing*.

Wedding Anniversary

Some say: "Familiarity breeds contempt."
But it can also feed forbearance
And a certain kind of kindness.
What was epiphany becomes assurance,
And a precious prize that's priceless.
The sharp edges blur as the days all rush,
Run and whir into weeks and months and years.
Where did they all go? We wonder,
Living in the linear. Our love grown
Fat in the soft circles of forgiveness…
While time is getting skinnier.

Summer Storm for Supplicants

The sky is full of omens.
The clouds form faces
And shadows dapple the stunted grass.

Like a legion of rowdy Romans
A phalanx of thunder passes
Over the mountains & into the basin.

Drench us in this weather.
Give us a rain to remember.
For we are scorched beyond endurance.
Our desperation shall be thy splendor.

Heavy Elements

The lightening rips
A seam of sky
Wide open:
Slashing a gash
Through night's
Wine dark manuscript.

And the stars are
The trillion eyes
Of an unseen god—
Each eye lit
Like a candle wick
To illuminate or ignite

The parchment
Of our hearts:
Our weeping wax—
And sticky pitch—
All our combustible
Bits and parts

That come from
The same stuff of stars—
(Or so I've been told).
Formed in the furnace
Of a cosmic bonfire:
4.6 *billion* years old.

At the Franciscan Retreat Center, Colorado Springs

As the deer pants for streams of water, so my soul pants for you, my God.
—Psalm 42:1

A congregation of devout deer
appeared over the hill
and came down to graze
on a Eucharist of leaves:

The new, green goodness
of God's good spring.

Initially, there was no rapture
just a rupture in my reverie.

I had no idea what might occur:
smoking my cigarette outside
like a thurifer.

It didn't seem to bother them though:
the smoke. They must have known
I wasn't a wildfire.
Just another man sacrificing himself
in the wilderness.

And then, with magnificent tenderness,
one of the deer got so near to me…
20 feet or less. We were now
in the same sanctuary of grass.

For some reason I looked away and
stretched out my left hand
thinking: "This too shall pass."

But it did not.

The deer approached without fear
his black nose nuzzled
my palm, the nostrils flaring.

And that was it.
Who blessed who I don't know.
But he left as gentle
as a penitent.

I Didn't Intend to End This with a Quote from Jaroslav Pelikan

Lately, I've grown tired
of the way I write…
weary of the bells that jingle
on a hell-bent sleigh ride
of black scribble
across the white snowfall
of the page.

I wince as Mother Goose
slams one door after another
in closure.
But I like it too:
The comfort of order.

No art without the discipline
of a well-watched border.

Transgression has become so common
as to become commonplace.

Use a rhymed couplet
and many editors are unforgiving.
But remember:

Tradition is the living faith of the dead—
traditionalism: the dead faith of the living.

About the Author

Among other things, Daniel has been an actor, a labor rights activist, the lead singer/lyricist for the Indie rock band Mining for Rain, and a poetry book reviewer for NewPages.com. His poems have appeared widely in journals and magazines, both online and in print, in Australia, the UK, and the U.S. Daniel has a BA in Religion Studies with a minor in Theater Arts from the College of Santa Fe and a Master of Divinity degree with a justice and peace studies concentration from The Iliff School of Theology in Denver. A member of the Colorado Poets Center, he is the author of two full-length poetry collections: *A Poet Playing Doctor* (2015) and *Plato Poetica* (spring, 2017), both published by White Violet Press, as well as a chapbook of children's poems entitled *Put on Your Silly Pants:* Poems for Children and Very Immature Adults (Daffydowndilly Press/Kelsay Books, fall, 2016) which won Honorable Mention in the 2017 Purple Dragonfly Book Awards for Children's Poetry. You can read more about Daniel at: poetdanielklawitter.wordpress.com

www.ingramcontent.com/pod-product-compliance
Lightning Source LLC
LaVergne TN
LVHW021625080426
835510LV00019B/2764